of the

guardians

Robert E. Ray

Copyright © 2025 by Robert E. Ray

All rights reserved. No part of this book may be used or reproduced by any means, graphic, electronic, or mechanical, including photocopying, recording, taping or by any information storage retrieval system without the written permission of the publisher, except the brief quotations embodied in critical articles and reviews.

For my brother and sister *guardians*
and our families.

The wicked flee when no man pursueth: but the righteous are bold as a lion.

—Proverbs 28:1

Accounting

> The one thing that doesn't abide by
> majority rule is a person's conscience.
> —Harper Lee, *To Kill a Mockingbird*

Atticus wakes my morality.
Rioters, some voters, hurl blue flames.
What's the will of the majority?—
Not the issue at hand. Vile, three names
spit in wind, spew splattered on our shields;
like acid rain it erodes the glass.
We serve, *we the people*, ideals.
No one reduces this promise to ash!
Brothers, sisters, keepers of the flame,
what the *guardians* tend shall remain.

Braving

> Never give up, for that is just the place and
> time that the tide will turn.
> —Harriet Beecher Stowe

Between that slave state of Kentucky
and the free state of Ohio lay
that big river, ice choked, white floes she,
Eliza, crossed, leap by leap, to save
Harry from chains, denied the promise—
The Declaration, Constitution.
    We probe and push the recruits; most pass
the basic class, one evolution.
Nobody's sure what's coming after.
    There's really no substitution—
no river, no heart we can measure.

Compassion

> Bearing the bandages, water and sponge,
> Straight and swift to my wounded I go…
> —Walt Whitman, *The Wound-Dresser*

Combat-care the war-mind reconciles.
We find softness in steel, our own flesh,
blood and bone. A godzillion damn times
the medic comes as we sleep, drills us.
To protect is to feel what must be
endured. "No one is coming," he shouts.
    We didn't get hit—it's our buddy,
a mother, a baby bleeding out—
and the tatted gangster who fired first.
We have one more tourniquet, one more
to save, oath to keep—just as we swore.

Duty

> Of my death, tell them I have done my duty.
> —Henry Joy McCracken

ebēre, from Latin, to *owe*. Your duty
is your calling. You owe yourself this:
Surrender to your humanity.

You know, "We are unworthy servants.
We've only done what was our duty"—
spelled out in the book of Luke, gospel.

So, you're in the clutch of the city
and you're the right fist, the apostle
for justice, the bearer of burden,
blessing, voice of reason, the chosen.

This is the cost, the gift of freedom.

Empathy

> Wherever there is a human being, there is
> an opportunity for a kindness.
> —Seneca

Edge of the inner city, the poor
beg for help, for those some neighbors hate.
Every block reeks of trash, booze, and fear.
     Solomon says, "Geography's fate."
That drunk, Noah, hasn't eaten for days,
since the city garbage trucks hauled out
what he and crows would've eaten in place—
flesh left on the bones, and the good fat.
     Jacob, eleven, delivers dope
for Joe, out on parole for the same.
Joe beats Mary. You're his—her last hope.

Fairness

> It's not fair, after all, to lick tigers so small.
> —Dr. Seuss, *I Can Lick 30 Tigers Today!*

F*airness*: "Just conduct; clearness of skin."
I read, *White's Modern Dictionary,*
1898. The paper's thin,
brittle, browning. I'm literary:
      Blindfolded lady, Justitia,
materializes on the paper—
goddess of justice. America,
her runaway wild child. Her power,
the sword. Her scales, our legal system.
      We don't touch her. We don't come near
her hands. Not a finger. Not a thumb.

Grit

> Out of the night that covers me,
> Black as the pit from pole to pole,
> I thank whatever gods there be
> For my unconquerable soul.
>   —William Ernest Henley, *Invictus*

Gilded bronze, casted war horse and rider
figures on monumental granite.
If you can reach her, you can touch her;
warm in dawn sun, the dew, still her grit.
  She demands this, relative hardness—
alloy. She'll test your composition,
durability. She'll ask, "Can you last?
  What's your content and your corrosion
resistance?" None of us is stainless,
steel or iron. If knocked down, if cut
will you rub dirt on it—and get up?

Honor

> Stern Lawgiver! yet thou dost wear
> The Godhead's most benignant grace...
> —William Wordsworth, *Ode to Duty*

Humility in the highest place. Your silence speaks the invisible mass. Doing the hard right. No witness. Count. How many Tuesdays remain till the end of the year, your career, life?

It's September 11th, again. This is the 254th day of the year—the Gregorian calendar (it's named after that Pope, the 13th). I look up. Each window frames a face I honor in the smoke.

Integrity

> Boldly they rode and well,
> Into the jaws of Death,
> Into the mouth of hell…
> —Alfred, Lord Tennyson, *The Charge of the
> Light Brigade*

I pray, swear faith to the ideal,
the American institution
that bears not one individual
face, not one color, not one faction.
      And this shall be your test, my brothers,
my sisters, to hold your oath sky-high
read the sacred words of the Founders
forward and backward. There is no *I*
      we serve. This is what Plato opposed—
mad democracy, the demagogues
who rise in their own fire and chaos.

Justice

>Through me you pass into the city of woe:
>Through me you pass into eternal pain:
>Through me among the people lost for aye.
>Justice the founder of my fabric moved
>   —Dante Alighieri, *The Divine Comedy*

Judas exacted his own justice.
We read Sophocles, *Antigone*
translated, and Milton, *Paradise Lost*,
Kafka, *The Trial*—arbitrary
systems and alienation. And King—
    the one who didn't appoint himself,
who spoke gospel one woman would sing;
contralto, who carried the name of
Jackson, owner of slaves, that hater
of natives. She, others, saved and bore
that first letter, and Jesus, *juror*.

Kindness

> Before you know what kindness really is
> you must lose things, feel the future
> dissolve in a moment,
> like salt in a weakened broth.
> —Naomi Shihab Nye, *Kindness*

Keats: "A loving-kindness for the great man's fame dwells here and there with people of no name, in noisome alley and in pathless wood." Did he see this state at his death? What have you lost, sister, brother, in the boil of this city?

    Don't raise your hand to touch another before you've exited the *alley*.
Come then—carry in your open palm
(never a fist) your authority.

    Brace yourself before you speak to them.

Loyalty

> Though I've belted you and flayed you,
> By the livin' Gawd that made you,
> You're a better man than I am, Gunga Din!
> —Rudyard Kipling, *Gunga Din*

Look, read what they wrote at our founding.
They signed their names—their eyes open.
This profession of arms, this calling
of guardians, is bond with vision.
  We hold, shoulder to shoulder. We stand
with all the others, as the public,
feet deep-rooted in his hallowed ground
among the strong, with the dying sick—
  allegiance tempered by truth our sword,
iron sharpened by iron. Conflict
won't divide us. Our bond is our word.

Mercy

> But mercy is above this sceptred sway;
> It is enthronèd in the hearts of kings,
> It is an attribute to God himself;
> —Wm. Shakespeare, *The Merchant of Venice*

Morning comes gray. Book of James, I read
"For judgment is without mercy to
one who has shown no mercy. Mercy
triumphs over judgment." But through who?
    I see the paradox: strength that chooses
restraint. We have power to punish.
And power to withhold. I witness
this, a gift given to the selfish—
the undeserving ones. Who am I
off and on the low road to hades?
I own nothing outright. I see why.

Nobility

> Those that I fight I do not hate,
> Those that I guard I do not love…
> —W.B. Yeats, *An Irish Airman Foresees his Death*

Nelson Mandela. One man to grieve
who did not—in a fractured nation,
from apartheid to democracy,
not revenge but reconciliation.
    Who will pry open and hold the door
of this great, ancient institution?
Will you step down, in, onto the floor,
level yourself, craft your very own
resolution, words, deeds of service?
    It is the mark of the guardian
on the heart: Greatness measured by grace.

Objectivity

> We stood by a pond that winter day,
> And the sun was white, as though chidden
> of God.
> —Thomas Hardy, *The Neutral Tones*

Oil on canvas, the Otto Dix one,

The Trench, art condemned by the Nazis,

confiscated, an exhibition

of *degenerate art*, believed lost.

      We must see the ghastly aftermath,

the detritus of war: charred ruins,

fragmentary bodies, every death.

      Each human is an institution.

I can do this—hold my emotion

in check, still see each face through the haze.

      I see bias. I smell the decay.

Patience

> I will keep still and wait like the night with
> starry vigil
> and its head bent low with patience.
> The morning will surely come, the darkness
> will vanish…
> — Rabindranath Tagore, *Patience*

Patience of *Job*? I know no such man.
I've witnessed strong men and women break

like fine blue China. More than wisdom

one needs to bridle urgency, take

a deep breath, ten, not rush to ruin.

We, the prudent, use time as a tool.

We avoid the trap, lure, temptation

of the quick, bad decision. We fall—

no, not to our training but our own

constitution. *We, the People*, treat

as people. Not *problems*. Never sheep.

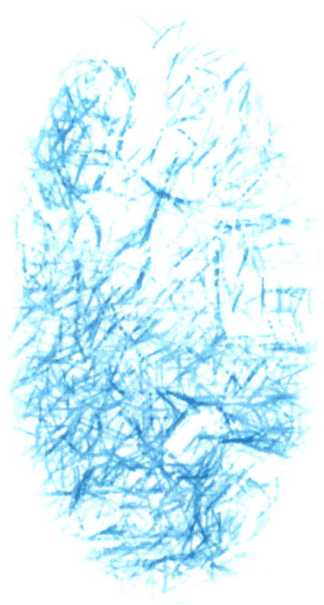

Quietude

> Speak your truth quietly and clearly;
> and listen to others,
> even the dull and the ignorant;
> they too have their story.
> —Max Ehrmann, *Desiderata*

Questions rise in stirred hot wind and rain.
Come to the room that holds the stillness
in the storm, that calm center, terrain
of higher ground, removed from chaos.

  She listens louder than any shout.
Do you recall her name? From Latin—
of clarity, justice, the quiet?

  Clara? The tight-lipped librarian?
Once, she asked me why I had two ears,
two eyes, two nostrils—only one mouth.

  I occupy the room no air stirs.

Resilience

> You may trod me in the very dirt
> But still, like dust, I'll rise.
> —Maya Angelou, *Still I Rise*

Resilience. I writhe in paradox.

When I can't deal with Christ, the Bible,

I go ancient, dig into the Greeks—

Prometheus, Titan, who defied

head gods to avail humanity.

He stole fire, gave it to the people.

Zeus ordered him bound to a boulder;

each day, liver exposed, an eagle

tore away more. Nightly, his liver

regenerated. Torment recurs

without end. I never surrender!

Sacrifice

> Between the crosses, row on row,
> That mark our place; and in the sky
> The larks, still bravely singing, fly
> Scarce heard amid the guns below.
> —John McCrae, *In Flanders Fields*

Squared, sitting, staring up, straight ahead
I study *The Annunciation*,
Mary's pale bowed head, her composed hands,
gesture of consent, and acceptance—

    the costly duty. Consecration
precedes self-giving. Scrawl your own name
in blood on the mirror. This nation
demands your life and offers no fame.

    Do you see it? Loss chosen for *love?*—
Giving what cannot be repaid.
Agape—the guardians don't speak of.

Transparency

> There's something happening here.
> What it is ain't exactly clear.
> There's a man with a gun over there.
> Telling me I got to beware.
>   —Buffalo Springfield, *For What It's Worth*

Transparent. I was advised to use
a different word, given the prefix. Exposure builds trust. So, I choose
to say *no*, live true to the word, "transmitting rays of light; clear." Here, between
this rock and hard place, I let the light
in, even when the rays sting and burn.

      I polish my shield, set it aside.
See, I'm a father to nothing new—
nothing since some celestial divine
said, "Let there be light." Yes, I see you.

Understanding

> I saw the land and the people, and my mind was made great
> With the sense of their sorrow and my own.
> —Edna St. Vincent Millay, *Renascence*

Underwater, I could see nothing.
Voices were muffled and my ears filled
with cold water and algae. Fishing,
zeroed on feeding rainbows, I slipped
in the mud, fell fast, head-first, face-down.

    It was an old river, new to me—
and the climate, and slope of the ground.

    A hen stared at me. Too big to eat—
she swallowed a nymph and shot upstream.

    Starved, I hit a drive-thru on Main Street.
That pickle-eye pollock near-choked me.

Valor

> Ever-returning spring, trinity sure to me
> you bring,
> Lilac blooming perennial and drooping star
> in the west,
> And thought of him I love.
> —Walt Whitman, *When Lilacs Last in the
> Dooryard Bloom'd*

Victory is one more break, no end—
a word, noun with no punctuation.
Whitman was speaking about Lincoln.
Roughly half the people hated him.

    There is no applause at funerals,
no medals for individuals
who serve us and don't die publicly;
admin staff, the wage-grade hourly,
the procurers of trucks, guns, body

    bags, toilet paper, and gasoline—
the gritty, bored, the necessary.

Wisdom

> A foolish consistency is the hobgoblin of
> little minds, adored by little statesmen and
> philosophers and divines.
> —Ralph Waldo Emerson, *Self Reliance*

White is the house I have transcended
and those facades of gods and lions.
Home is a mountain-top stone cabin;
over the mantle, antlers and guns.
Oak rockers face the fire and bourbon.
    Resurrected Lincoln & Emerson,
though teetotalers, visit. I drain
their jammed brains and learn that stamina
on the stump and at the podium—
when to speak and even more when to
    shush, take copious notes, and listen.

Xenial Spirit

> Give me your tired, your poor,
> Your huddled masses yearning to breathe free,
> The wretched refuse of your teeming shore.
> —Emma Lazarus, *The New Colossus*

Xanthic, the glow, Room 716—
the Louvre, Reni's *The Abduction
of Helen*; Paris, that punk Trojan
prince, kidnapping the wedded Helen
violating the domain of *Zeus
Xenios*, sparking the Trojan War.

They destroyed his city. Lessons
rise in light, like the Phoenix. The fire
the transformation—not the bird's rise
from ash. Once, we were "wretched refuse"
washed ashore—an old story of Grace.

In memory of Grace Ray (1892-1972)

Yielding

> They send me to eat in the kitchen
> When company comes,
> But I laugh,
> And eat well,
> And grow strong.
> Langston Hughes, I, Too

You've approached that fork in the road.
I know the spot, view this time of year,

aroma of the corn, red arrowhead-

shaped sign, pointed down; October air

crisp, cool, of decayed leaves, woodsmoke.

You know something's dying, something's dead

along the road because your window

is down. You used to know the field's yield—

just how many bushels per acre

the old man got from the soil he broke—

the farm you now guard for some banker.

Zeal

> Zeal should not outrun discretion.
> —Aesop, *The Thirsty Pigeon*

Zoomed, zeroed on the evildoers
you radio your *10-20*, watch—
wait, look out for your back up, troopers,
town marshal, past the scrolling bank clock.

You're a rookie, "bit overzealous,"
the prosecutor says days later.
And your sergeant calls you a "FNG."
Another one says the words after.

Now, your purpose tempers your passion.
You've lost the spark and glow—not the fire.
What was ore is cold-sharpened iron.

Amygdala

> Someone I loved once gave me a box full
> of darkness. It took me years to understand
> that this, too, was a gift.
> —Mary Oliver, *The Uses of Sorrow*

Luna eyes the neoclassical
house, lights out, grid down. One squatter
clasps the shutters, bolts the doors. Total
blackout. One ray breaks through, spills under.
Rain dumps more in the engorged river.
More squatters come; they share their Wonder
bread and booze. One says, "Eat and drink this."
    Orange & sweet—it tastes like prison
hooch. I know better than to listen.
No one makes sense this hour in this room.
    Fear's the swift legs of intuition.

Art: The Museo Nacional Centro
de Arte Reina Sofía in Madrid?
The Museum of Modern Art? No.
New York, 1980? Who painted
that Basque town? War. Pablo Picasso,
his blue period? Nevertheless—

    there are striking similarities;
mustiness of museums, faint light,
old-school snooty, blue-blood snobbishness
behind these whitewashed walls, the rise—

    the fall of Palladian columns.

Underestimated. Me. The air's May:
floral, buzzing, fragrant, less bitter
morning and evening. Her name is Mya,
    the *illegal alien* wetting one ear.
"Look far left. See the mad bull, black bulk,
white head? Tell me about your *market*.
You ever seen one express such shock,
horrors that engulf him? He's prime cut."
    I like her wit. I wasn't born last night.
"Now, look underneath. See the woman
clutching the stray cat? She's an orphan."

Right, Mya points down. A prone soldier.
Disjointed. Disembodied. Sapphire.
One palm holds a poppy—half saber

the other. Uncanny the color.

Above it all, a glass bulb dangles.
"God gives us this to see the chaos—

namely, war, destruction, lunacy.

We've grown, advanced; we're technically

better at slaughtering each other."

Sun lights a silver streak in her hair.
"Now go love your sister and brother."

Every pane is a portal, madness
on the periphery. The center
holds because—yes, there is evidence
of life—abundance and revere.
      I hear the chain and shackle rattle,
right ankle and foot free, and the left,
raw from resistance—hardness of scale,
bondage forged centuries ago. Guilt
and shame are not the same. We bleed out
from dissimilar wounds, different
parts of the same body: head, heart, foot.

Night, I come-to. The room's yellow—
truly sweet yellow, like goldenrod,
the ditches, and those fields of tobacco.
She's jabbering in her sleep, half-mad-
Appalachian-Pentecostal,
knee-deep in the undammed brown water.
She swears she won't drink it when she goes
down, where the doves and purple clouds blur,
where voices are muffled. So, I share
my dream— not of *Guernica*. It's pure
amygdala. "Take my hand," I say.

"I will lead us out. I know the way."

In my end is my beginning.
—T. S. Eliot, *Four Quartets*

Author Note on Form

If you've reached this page and not yet figured out the particular form, perhaps the content and meaning kept you from focusing on those technical qualities. Because poetry must have melody and meaning to distinguish itself from prose, I paid close attention to those elements in this collection. In addition to addressing a range of virtues and values, A to Z, I also kept each line to nine syllables, and each poem to 11 lines (not including the poem titles). This was done to honor our guardians, particularly those who served on September 11, 2001, and the years since, protecting this nation and its people.

In addition to the date itself, I found even more depth in those numbers. For example, September 11th is the 254th day of the year, leaving 111 days to the end of the year. For millennia, three lines and the Roman numeral III have had spiritual significance in many religions, including Christianity. Further, in Luke 15:4, part of Jesus' Parable of the Lost Sheep, He asks: "What man of you, having a hundred sheep, if he has lost one of them, does not leave the ninety-nine in the open country and go after the lost one until he finds it?" Why does this matter? Each poem is 11 lines, nine syllables in each line, for 99 syllables in each poem. We will never be whole if even one is absent.

Thank you for reading—and for the gift of your time.

Robert E. Ray
Georgia, U.S.A.
October 2025

Finally, be strong in the Lord and in his mighty power. Put on the full armor of God, so that you can take your stand against the devil's schemes.

—Ephesians 6:10-11

More to Read

Sir Robert Peel's Policing Principles

Sir Robert Peel established the London Metropolitan Police Force in 1829. He is widely considered the "Father of Modern Policing." His commissioners established nine policing principles that remain relevant.

1. To prevent crime and disorder, as an alternative to their repression by military force and severity of legal punishment.

2. To recognize always that the power of the police to fulfill their functions and duties is dependent on public approval of their existence, actions and behavior, and on their ability to secure and maintain public respect.

3. To recognize always that to secure and maintain the respect and approval of the public means also the securing of the willing cooperation of the public in the task of securing observance of laws.

4. To recognize always that the extent to which the cooperation of the public can be secured diminishes proportionately the necessity of the use of physical force and compulsion for achieving police objectives.

5. To seek and preserve public favor, not by pandering to public opinion, but by constantly demonstrating absolute impartial service to law, in complete independence of policy, and without regard to the justice or injustice of the substance of individual laws, by ready offering of individual

service and friendship to all members of the public without regard to their wealth or social standing, by ready exercise of courtesy and friendly good humor, and by ready offering of individual sacrifice in protecting and preserving life.

6. To use physical force only when the exercise of persuasion, advice and warning is found to be insufficient to obtain public cooperation to an extent necessary to secure observance of law or to restore order, and to use only the minimum degree of physical force which is necessary on any particular occasion for achieving a police objective.

7. To maintain at all times a relationship with the public that gives reality to the historic tradition that the police are the public and that the public are the police, the police being only members of the public who are paid to give full-time attention to duties which are incumbent on every citizen in the interests of community welfare and existence.

8. To recognize always the need for strict adherence to police-executive functions, and to refrain from even seeming to usurp the powers of the judiciary of avenging individuals or the State, and of authoritatively judging guilt and punishing the guilty.

9. To recognize always that the test of police efficiency is the absence of crime and disorder, and not the visible evidence of police action in dealing with them.

5 U.S. Code § 3331 - Oath of office

An individual, except the President, elected or appointed to an office of honor or profit in the civil service or uniformed services, shall take the following oath: "I, AB, do solemnly swear (or affirm) that *I will support and defend the Constitution of the United States* against all enemies, foreign and domestic; that *I will bear true faith and allegiance to the same*; that I take this obligation freely, without any mental reservation or purpose of evasion; and that I will well and faithfully discharge the duties of the office on which I am about to enter. So help me God."

(Pub. L. 89–554, Sept. 6, 1966, 80 Stat. 424.)

International Association of Chiefs of Police Policing Oath of Honor

On my honor, I will never betray my integrity, my character, or the public trust. I will treat all individuals with dignity and respect and ensure that my actions are dedicated to ensuring the safety of my community and the preservation of human life. I will always have the courage to hold myself and others accountable for our actions. I will always maintain the highest ethical standards and uphold the values of my community, and the agency I serve.

International Association of Chief of Police. Retrieved October 16, 2025, from
https://www.theiacp.org/sites/default/files/2025-06/246910_IACP_Oath_of_Honor_11x8.5_p1%20%281%29.pdf

If you love this book, please share it with fellow guardians, friends, family members, neighbors, strangers—and those who do not understand this calling.

Robert E. Ray's poetry has been published by Rattle, The Ekphrastic Review, Wild Roof Journal, The Wee Sparrow Poetry Press, The Nuthatch, The Muleskinner Journal, Beyond Words Literary Magazine, and numerous print and digital anthologies. He is a graduate of Eastern Kentucky University. Robert lives in rural southeast Georgia.

Comments on this poetry collection:

For those who stand between chaos and the rest of us, this book speaks their language.

A moral anatomy of service, rendered in the precision of craft and the heat of conscience.

When duty demands everything, these poems keep the ledger of the heart.

Brave, disciplined, and merciful: a modern liturgy for public life.

Honor without sentimentality; grief without surrender.

Robert E. Ray's *Of the Guardians* is a rigorous, luminous sequence of poems that names and remakes the moral vocabulary of public service. Arranged A to Z, each compact poem is a disciplined jewel that shines a light on courage, mercy, duty, and grief with a voice exacting and tender. These are poems of bearing: witnesses to the small mercies and vast costs of keeping watch, poems that move from street corners and morgues to county halls and sacred memory. Drawing on classical allusion, scriptural resonance, and hard-won observation, Ray holds a mirror to those who answer the call and to the nation they serve. Stark imagery and quietly searing argument converge in an ethical liturgy that honors sacrifice, demands accountability, and insists that the public trust is a living thing. *Of the Guardians* is elegy and education, prayer and indictment, a book for readers who want language tough enough to name danger and luminous enough to restore faith.

www.ingramcontent.com/pod-product-compliance
Lightning Source LLC
Chambersburg PA
CBHW041524090426
42737CB00038B/110